Avast

POCKET

BOOK OF

PIRATES

Cina Qedesh Bolton

The Pocket Book of Pirates

ISBN 1845679997
Printed by Antony Rowe
Chippenham, Wiltshire.

www.bandwagonpublishing.com

For Zeke

Cover layout and illustrations by PaW
www.23-5.co.uk

Contents:

'Barnacles' see page 22

Top Ten Real Pirates

1/ EDWARD TEACH

Teach A.K.A Blackbeard was born in
Bristol in the 1680's.
Hated and feared by all he encountered,
his smoky black beard tied with ribbons,
his overbearing height and his fearsome
growling voice made him
an intimidating force.
It is said that Teach is the originator of
pirate talk bringing his west country
drawl to the high seas, with his ARRs and
never puttin' a G on the end of anythin'.
It is also fabled that he invented drinking
games, with a loaded pistol and a bottle
of rum, it was more drink or
die than drink and think.
He killed any pirate, sailor or shipmate
that got in his way, making him the most
notorious pirate of all time.

☠

2/ MARY READE

This kick-ass female pirate first dressed
as a man to get her hands on her
father's inheritance.
The historical tom-boy quickly realised
she quite liked being a man and kept up
her cross-dressing and joined the
military. Reade excelled as a swordsman
and in hand-to-hand combat, but soon
searched for a more exciting life on the
high seas. She cursed like a man, fought
like a man and drank like a true pirate.

With her pal Anne Bonny they often
defended their ship from attack as an axe
and sword wielding duo because the male
pirates were asleep or too drunk to fight.

☠

3/ BARTHOLOMEW ROBERTS

Roberts A.K.A Black Bart was born
in Pembrokeshire in the 1680's.
This Welsh buccaneer was statistically
the most successful pirate of all time,
capturing and raiding well over
400 ships in his career.
Always clean-shaven and immaculately
dressed, Black Bart was the most
dapper of all the pirates.
A teetotal Captain who discouraged
drinking amongst the crew, he even
organised musical evenings for them.
His excellent manners and soberness did
not help when he got shot dead in the
neck by a great big cannonball.

A successful pirate but a boring pirate.

4/ ANNE BONNY

This Irish outlaw reputedly stabbed a
servant girl in the stomach with a table
knife when she was just 13.
She turned to piracy when she was
wooed away from her husband by
'Calico' Jack Rackham and they
cruised the Caribbean
plundering all they could.
Bonny hadn't realised her shipmate
Mary Reade was a woman until
she walked in on
her when she was topless.
They soon became firm friends and a
formidable fighting force.
In 1720 after many furious battles Anne
and Mary were arrested, but escaped
execution because they were pregnant.
The rest of the crew got hanged.

☠

5/ EDWARD LOWE

Londoner Lowe is a good contender
for cruelest pirate ever!
He drove his crew to mutiny with his
violent and irrational temper.
His brutal regime left the occupants
of the Caribbean and the Azores
quaking in their boots.
Known for his creative torture methods,
his favourite one was cutting off a
victim's lips, cooking them whilst the
lipless enemy watched, then forcing the
victim to eat them....nice!

He was, however, the first Captain to
offer pirate insurance, giving the
unlucky crew member 600 pieces of eight
for each limb lost during battle.
(you got nothing for lost lips)

☠

6/ FRANCIS L'OLLONAIS

This French pirate is another contender
for cruelest pirate ever.
L'ollonais and his men raped and
pillaged their way around the
Caribbean in a hellish fashion.
Capable of killing his whole crew
just to prove a point, his favourite
torture was tightening a rope around a
victim's neck until their eyes popped
out of their sockets.
One unfortunate Spaniard got his heart
cut out with a cutlass and L'ollonais
gnawed on it there and then.
If he ever got in a sticky situation, he
would cover himself in a shipmate's blood
and pretend to be dead.
He was finally captured by cannibalistic
Indians in the Gulf of Darien,
who ate him!

☠

7/ HOWELL DAVIS

Welsh Davis was a mentor for the
very famous Back Bart.
He passed himself on to many as a
law-abiding pirate hunter, but he was
really keeping all the loot to himself.
A master of deception, he once captured
one French ship full of loot.
Soon after, a larger twenty-four gun ship
came into view, so he dressed the first
ship's crew as pirates and
raised a jolly roger.

The large ship, thinking it was up against
a fleet of pirates quickly surrendered and
both boats were plundered before they
could say "Shiver me timbers!"

☠

8/ JACK RACKHAM

Rackham, A.K.A Calico Jack, is most famous for having Mary Reade and Anne Bonny on his ship disguised as men. A former Quartermaster on the Neptune, Rackham organised a mutiny against their lacklustre Captain, Charles Vane. After a few years of piracy he begged the King's pardon and vowed to a trouble free life on dry land.
Not long later he met Anne Bonny, a married woman, and they ran off together for a new life on the seas. He worked the Bahamas, Jamaica and the coast of Cuba with his female bodyguards as backup.

Jack was finally captured and hanged in 1721.

9/ WILLIAM KIDD

Scottish born Kidd spent twenty years as a seaman before ending up in New York. Once there he married wealthy twice-widowed teenager Sarah Bradley Cox-Oort and built up a name for himself around the City.

He struck a pact with wealthy governors and, funded by the government, set sail to attack the well-known pirates of the day and return with the loot.

In 1697 his backers were nervous their identity would be revealed. They pulled out of the deal and covered up any trace of the dealings.

Kidd then became the proper bloodthirsty pirate he is known as today.

☠

He was, however, dogged with bad luck, a string of mouldy boats, cholera-ridden crews, leaky hulls and bad timing all lead to his crew deserting him.

10/ HENRY EVERY

Plymouth born Every, A.K.A Long Ben
or Benjamin Bridgeman, is one of
the most celebrated pirates.
A former slave trader, Every took his
first ship 'The Fancy' by storming her
when the captain was drunk.
His well-planned reign continued,
storming ships in night raids with
carefully executed attacks.
Every and his crew stole the ultimate
booty when they plundered a treasure
ship belonging to the Mughal Emperor of
India, reputedly containing 5 million
rupees. Henry did the sensible thing and
retired before being caught and hanged.
Stories tell of him living out his final
years in Bideford, Devon.

☠

Top Ten Fictional Pirates

1/ CAPTAIN PUGWASH

Sailing the high seas on his ship
'The Black Pig'
Pugwash and his crew embarked on
brilliant adventures in the T.V series
and books by John Ryan.
Contrary to popular belief the characters
Seaman Stains, Master Bates and Roger
the cabin boy never existed.
They were actually called
Master Mate, Tom the cabin boy and
Willy.

2/ LONG JOHN SILVER

Silver was Quartermaster to Captain
John Flint in Robert Louis Stephenson's
'Treasure Island'.
Also known as 'Barbecue', he ticks all the
pirate boxes, a hardworking villain with
a parrot and one leg!

☠

3/ CAPTAIN HOOK

From J.M Barrie's 'Peter Pan', this
stylish buccaneer had a proper
hook and everything.
He had the full-on pirate look with the
red coat, tri-cornered hat and
flowing locks.
A bit of a let-down on the villain part
when he topped himself by jumping
into a crocodile's mouth because he was
scared of a clock!

4/ CAPTAIN JACK SPARROW

Rolling Stones guitarist Keith Richards
inspired this cult character
played by Johnny Depp in
'Pirates of the Caribbean'.
His boozy swagger and dirty face has
made him popular with young
pirate-loving ladies across the world.

☠

5/ ONE EYED WILLIE

Trapped in a cave by the British armada
in 1632 with all of his treasure,
he managed to carve an intricate entry to
his cave to stop anyone getting their
hands on his precious loot.
Littered with booby traps, trap
doors and even a 'death organ' made out
of old bones, Willie made it virtually
impossible to get to him or his booty.
But he couldn't get himself out, could he?
Some kids went to rescue him in the
1980's, but he was already dead by then.

6/ THE MINIPIRATES

Walter Moers has created the ultimate
ridiculous pirates in his book
'The 13 ½ Lives of Captain Bluebear'.
Six-inch tall, eye-patch wearing pirates
with hooks on both hands and pegs on
both legs, not exactly a force to be
reckoned with, but are very persistent!

☠

7/ RED RACKHAM

Loosely based on 'Calico' Jack Rackham, this pirate first features in the Tintin story 'The Secret of the Unicorn'. Captain Haddock's Ancestor Francis had killed this evil pirate many years ago and Tintin and Haddock set off on a mission to retrieve the sunken treasure. Good clean pirate fun!

8/ DREAD PIRATE ROBERTS

From the book ' The Princess Bride'. The hero of the book, Westley, is released from the clutches of Dread Pirate Roberts (real name Ryan) after Westley tells an enduring story of needing to return to his true love.

☠

9/ ERROL FLYNN

Remembered more as a swashbuckling
pirate than a real person,
Flynn filled his life with fighting,
drinking and women. Occasionally
stopping to fight with drunken women.

10/ STEVE THE PIRATE

This chap from the film 'Dodgeball' was
man on the outside, pirate on the inside.
His is a glorious tale of triumph over
adversity and shows that however
much persecution you take, you have
to be true to your heart.
Your cold, drunk, pirate heart.

*The most rubbish fictional pirate
award goes to.....*
THE PIRATES OF PENZANCE
Pirates singing comedy opera? Not
on my watch matey!

Pirate Dictionary

(All the knowledge you need
for a life on the high seas)

ADDLE ~
From the Old English for pool of excrement, meaning muddled or messed up. "Me brain be addled on this rum."

AHOY ~
Common pirate exclamation.
Alexander Graham Bell suggested 'Ahoy!' as the standard telephone greeting, but unfortunately it didn't catch on.

ALBATROSS ~
Killing or harming this legendary bird would be unforgivable to any sailor, coining the phrase
'An albatross round your neck'.

ARMADILLO ~
Spanish for a small armada (fleet of ships). Also the answer to the joke: What is a pirate's favourite animal?

ARR ~
Not many languages have a word that means nothing yet is used for everything.

AVAST! ~
Exclamation meaning Stop That!
"Avast me hearties, that there biscuit ain't ne'er goin' to be soggy"

AXE ~
The long handled axe came in very handy for breaking down cabin doors on enemy ships, cutting gang ropes and splicing foes in 'alf!

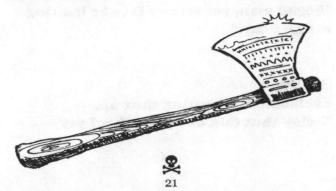

AYE ~
Yes.

AYE AYE CAP'N! ~
Best said when the captain wears an eye patch.

BARNACLE ~
A type of crustacean that attaches itself to salt~ridden timber.

BEGAD! ~
By God!
"Begad man, yer scurvy face be looking rough t'day."

BELAY ~
Exclamation meaning shut up.
"Belay that talk or I'll keelhaul ye!"

BELAYING PIN ~

Like a big heavy wooden tent peg used to secure the rigging.
These little fellas are everywhere and are the perfect size and weight for clubbing your enemy to death.

BILGE ~

The ship's hull and keel fill with bilge water which is normally pretty dirty stuff.
"Ye' be talking bilge," would mean "Bullshit." Add on words to make authentic insults eg. bilge-suckin', bilge-lickin', Ye' hairy bilge-lovin' bastard.

BLACK SPOT ~

Placing the 'black spot' on another marks them for death. While pirates enjoyed insulting each other for fun, it gets serious when this is mentioned.

☠

BLEED THE MONKEY ~
To sneakily remove rum from a keg with a straw.

BLIMEY! ~
From the old English expression 'God blind me'. As pirates normally just have the one eye anyway maybe they shouldn't be chancing it with this expression.

BLOODY FLUX ~
Dysentery. Many pirates were plagued by this illness leaving the victims with bloody diarrhea and severe rectal pain. "AARR, me arse hurts!"

BLUE MONDAY ~
The day the punishments got handed out.

BOATSWAIN ~
pron. Bosun. These guys looked after the rigging and anchors and were normally the first to get the blame.

BOOTY ~
Brilliant things plundered from ships.

BOUCAN ~
Like a mini cutlass for killing wild boar. Really comes in handy in a fight when you've lost your sword and axe.

BOUNTY ~
The reward for capturing a pirate, or a delicious chocolate 'n' coconut treat.

BOWSPRIT ~
The big wooden spar (long pole) pointing forward over the bows of the ship.

BRETHEREN OF THE COAST ~
A group of Caribbean pirates in the 1640's from different ships who formed a pact not to attack and steal from each other. A few years down the line they were all attacking and stealing from each other.

BROADSIDE ~
To simultaneously fire all your guns on one side of your ship, or a particularly meaty wench.

BUCCANEER ~
From the French boucan meaning to barbecue. Buccaneers are the kings of the pirates. Based in the Caribbean these hard drinking, hard living, dirty-faced fellas love nothing more than some good shanty songs, loose women and a wild boar grillin' on the barbecue.
Sounds like May Bank holiday in Romford.

BUCKO ~
A friendly way of calling someone an idiot.

BY THE POWERS! ~
A favourite Long John Silver exclamation. Use it yourself by adding your favourite celebrity pirate..." By the Powers of John Prescott" !

CABIN BOY ~
Contrary to popular belief most cabin boys were spotty, scurvy ridden oiks, not beautiful young girls dressing as boys to escape their drunken fathers and live an exciting life on the high seas. Sorry.

☠

CACKLING FARTS ~
Eggs.

CAP'N ~
Because pirates were normally drunk, a lot of words were shorter. It is also easier to fit it into the verse of a sea shanty.

CAREEN ~
A way of 'dry docking' the ship for cleaning or repair. The ship is beached on it side and worked on, this leaves her open for attack but can lead to some really cool beach fights with flares a' blazin' and th' clash o' swords.

CAT 'O' NINE TAILS ~
Leather-bound whip with nine knotted chords known as the 'cat'.
"Belay ye' bilge ye' scurvy rat or ye'll feel the wrath of me cat."

CATGUT SCRAPER ~
The fiddler in the ship's band,
"That Nigel Kennedy's a right catgut scraper."

CHASE ~
The ship being pursued.
"Arr, she be givin' good chase."

CHEST ~
The best thing to keep your treasure in.

CHIP LOG ~

A pirate's speedometer. A length of line knotted at equal intervals and weighted at the end. Also handy for garroting your enemies to death.

COCKED HAT ~

The traditional three-cornered hat. An essential accessory for all Captains.

CORSAIR ~

This way of saying pirate is like an estate agent saying 'cosy' when really he means 'tiny and damp'.

CROW'S NEST ~

The highest observation point on the vessel. The least drunk pirate with two good eyes and the loudest voice would normally end up there.

CUTLASS ~
(Cutlash) Traditional pirate weapon.
The bigger and shinier the better.

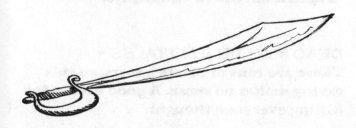

CUT~THROAT ~
Most lawless pirates of all, plundering
and looting from anyone. Ruthless.

DAVY JONES' LOCKER ~
The bottom of the sea. Davy Jones is often
referred to as the 'devil of the sea' and
sending a victim to his locker means
killing him, chucking him overboard and
letting his evil pirate soul rot forever.

DEADLIGHTS ~
Strong wooden shutters also meaning eyes.
"Begad man, use ye' deadlights."

DEAD MEN TELL NO TALES ~
There are tons of pirate ghosts, so this saying makes no sense. A good excuse for killing everyone though!

DEAD RECKONING ~
An exact calculation of where the ship is heading using knot speed, wind, currents and compass readings.
Accurate after the first bottle of rum, but then normally descends into blindly sailing around drunk and attacking people.

DOG ~
One of the nicer insults. 'Salty Seadog' is almost praise.

DOUBLOON ~
One of these was worth 16 pieces of eight. So it was worth 128... confused?

DUGOUT ~
A canoe made of a hollowed out tree. "Arrr, ye' ship be ney better than a dugout."

ESCUDO ~
Eight of these gold coins is equal to a doubloon. Just to add to the confusion.

FAIR WINDS! ~
And 'Godspeed!' Pirates tend to say
goodbye like this to their friends.
They don't need to say goodbye to their
foes because they kill them.

FATHOM ~
A way of measuring how deep the ocean
is. A fathom is the length of a sailor's
outstretched arms.
Never underestimate the technical mind
of a pirate.

FEED THE FISH ~
This is what happens when a pirate
throws you dead into the sea. Gangsters
are more polite about this and refer to it
as 'Sleeping with the fishes'.

FIDDLERS GREEN ~
Pirate heaven.

FIGUREHEAD ~
Carved figure at the front of the ship.
Normally a busty mermaid, Yarr!

FIRESHIP ~
An unwanted ship filled with explosives
and a lit slow match. The boat would
then be set adrift toward an enemy ship
to cause a massive explosion.

FLOGGING ~
Fierce caning of whipping with the 'cat'
as punishment, not to be confused with
BBC1's 'Flog It'.

FLOTSAM ~
The floating debris around a wrecked ship.
"Arr the cook's stew be looking like flotsam and bilge."

GANGWAY! ~
Polite way of saying "Out of me way or get a cutlass through ye' heart!"

GAOL ~
Jail. The only country that still uses this old English word is Australia, which ironically is one big prison full of pirate descendants.

GENTLEMEN 'O' FORTUNE ~
Nice way of saying pirate.

GIBBET~
After being caught and hanged, pirates would be displayed in this iron cage as a warning to others.

GOUT ~
Rife amongst pirates and made worse by only drinking alcohol and eating fish.

GRAPPLING IRON ~
Hook on a rope to aid the boarding of enemy ships. Also good for gouging out eyes.

GROG ~
Rum. (Or any booze they could get their dirty pirate hands on.)

GROWLER ~
Small island or part of an iceberg that has come loose.
"Growler, dead ahead!"

GRUB ~
Food. Mostly pickled in rum.

GULLY ~
Knife used as an eating utensil, often hidden up a sleeve and used in the first stages of mutiny.

HARDTACK ~
Stale, rock~hard biscuits. Hated by all who sailed the seas.
Slightly better dipped in rum.

HELM ~
Ship's wheel.

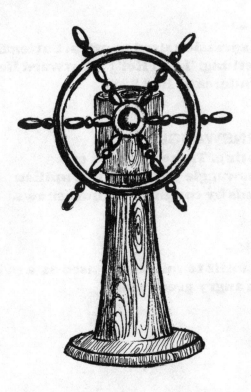

☠

HEMPEN HALTER ~
The hangman's noose.

HO! ~
An expression used to attract attention to something: 'Land Ho!' ; 'Westward Ho!' ; 'Thundercats, Ho ! '

HORNSWAGGLE ~
Cheating. These days you can hornswaggle your way to a million pounds by coughing on quiz shows.

HULK ~
Ship unfit to sail that is used as a prison, or an angry green man.

JACK KETCH ~

Legendary hangman. Jack was either clumsy or very sadistic as his hanging and beheadings often ended up in horrific situations.
His ropes would often break or he would chop the wrong part off. This was a very humiliating end for a pirate and Jack's name has lived on in insult form.

JACK TAR ~

Sailors were called this for slicking back their pony-tailed hair with tar. This method is still used by the bouncers of 'Jumpin' Jacks' nightclub in Gloucester.

JETSAM ~

Things that get thrown overboard to lighten the ship if it is in trouble. Cabin boys, the Captain's wife, but never weapons, Arr!

JIB ~

Large triangular sail, this would be cut thin by Spanish and French buccaneers. English pirates didn't like the cut of them.

JIB (HANG THE) ~

To 'Hang the jib' means to pull a sulky face. For an example of this look at men waiting outside Top Shop on a Saturday afternoon for their girlfriends.

JOLLY ROGER ~

Why don't people have their own flags anymore? It should be law.

KEELHAUL ~
Punishment by dragging a shipmate from one side of the keel to the other. If you don't end up dead from this punishment your flesh and bones are ripped apart by the barnacle ridden hull and your lungs are filled with salty water.
Even worse, you are left utterly disillusioned by pirate life and doubting your school career officer's choice.

KISS THE GUNNER'S DAUGHTER ~
(Marry the gunner's daughter)
Actually means being bent over a cannon and flogged 'till you bleed. Very misleading!

LANDLUBBER ~
Unless ye' be a pirate, they be talking 'bout ye'.

LEAGUE ~
One of these is equal to 3 nautical miles (1852 metres). But '111200000 Nautical Miles under the sea' just doesn't sound as exciting.

LETTERS OF MARQUE ~
A job list given to Privateers to retrieve goods from enemy merchants. Or permission from the government to sail the seas killin' 'n' robbin'.

LILY~LIVERED ~
Fainthearted sailors. Usually used to describe a pirate who absconded from a eating victim's body parts.

☠

LINE ~
When used as part of the rigging it's a line. When it's not being used it's called a rope, don't ask me why. Also good for hanging traitors.

LOOKOUT ~
"Lookout, thar be a giant octopus boarding ship!"

MAROON ¹ ~
What happens when you mix red and blue together.

MAROON ² ~
A pirate way of killing a shipmate or Captain. It can feel a bit weird impaling someone you know so well through the heart with a cutlass, so the easy way out is to leave them on a desert island with no water (rum) or food.

MATEY ~
Piratical way of addressing someone, not necessarily friendly. To this day if you hear "What are you looking at, matey?" in the Bristol docks its gonna end in trouble.

ME ~
My.

MEASURED FOR CHAINS ~
A treat meaning sizing someone up for the gibbet. "Belay that chatter or ye' be measured for chains"

ME HEARTIES ~
Next time you enter a room/bus/place of worship/boardroom full of people try shouting "Ahoy Me Hearties". *This* is how to get respect.

MOSES' LAW ~
This punishment is pretty close to a death sentence. The offender would receive 39 lashes to his bare back.

NO QUARTER ~
Hardcore pirates had this printed on their flags to say "Don't even bother surrendering, we show no mercy and we want to have a bloody good fight and kill you all."

ON THE ACCOUNT ~
Turning to a life of piracy.

PIECE OF EIGHT ~
A silver coin worth eight Reals, chopped into eight pieces with an axe becomes 'pieces of eight'. But if you cut up two, it is equal to a doubloon.
Next time you need change for the bus, just tear a tenner into quarters... if it's good enough for the pirates....

PIGGIN ~
Small bucket with a metal handle and bottom used for bailing out water. A last resort weapon, but easily swung into an enemy's face.

PILLAGE ~
To leave a ship empty and wrecked.

POOP DECK ~
Raised deck at the aft (rear) of the ship. Many people think this is the toilet on board, it is not. Pirates just do their wees and poos over the edge because they are dirty.

PORT ~
Opposite of starboard.

POWDER MONKEY ~
The boy who looks after the gunpowder.
Those people blaming rap culture for gun
crimes should really look back into
history a bit.

POXY, POX ~
"Gang-way ye' poxy faced biscuit~eater."

PRESSGANG ~
Being forced into service on a pirate ship.
Also brilliant 80's telly.

PRIVATEER ~
Semi-legal pirates working under
government orders, they still got to do all
the good stuff but didn't get told off
(hanged) for it.

ROPE'S END ~
If the cat 'o' nine tails wasn't to hand and a fast flogging was in need, you would feel the 'rope's end' (also called a fag end).

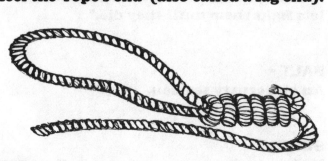

RUM ~
Tipple of choice, or a strange person. "He be a rum fellow, no parrot and 20/20 vision, Arrr!"

RUN A RIG ~
To play a trick. Often shipmates would play tricks on their captain by talking in a posh voice or having a wash. They would be hanged for it.

SAIL HO! ~
Exclamation meaning another vessel is in view.
"Sail Ho, there's a ship on the horizon, lets fight them until they die."

SALT ~
An old, crusty seaman.

SCURVY ~
Modern sailors now combat this disease with opal fruits, but pirates were lacking vitamin C. Symptoms of scurvy are having a peg leg, wearing an eye patch and a parrot and saying ARRRRR a lot.

SCUTTLE ~
To sink your own boat. A lot of teenage boys do this.

☠

SEA DOG ~
Another way of saying crusty seaman.

SHANTY ~
A sailor's song to work along to. Sadly missed in offices across the country.

SHARK BAIT ~
"Swab them decks or ye'll be shark bait."

SHIVER ME TIMBERS! ~
Originally meaning, 'Well, chop up me wooden leg'.
This is now a generic pirate exclamation.

SINK ME! ~
"Sink me if ye' ain't th' prettiest mermaid I ever clapped my eye on."
"I'm not a mermaid, I'm a dolphin and that's my blow hole."

SMARTLY ~
Meaning quickly, not cleverly.
Pirates do things fast and badly.

SPLICE THE MAIN BRACE ~
The captain would ceremoniously splice
up a tapered rope to show that extra rum
rations had been issued as a reward for a
good day's pillaging.
A drinking session would ensue with
shanty singing and a damn good scrap.

ST. FIACRE ~
The patron Saint of syphilis,
hemorrhoids and venereal disease.
A well-known figure on the seas.

STARBOARD ~
Opposite of port.

☠

SUTLER ~
(Chandler) One stop shop for all your pirate needs. These port merchants loved to barter with the buccaneers and came out of the deal better off (or dead).

SWAB, SWABBIE ~
A mop made of a stick and some rope ends. A swabbie was the lowest in the ship's pecking order.
Modern day swabbies can be found in shopping centers across the country acting like security guards just because they've got a walkie-talkie.

SWEATS, THE ~
Smallpox or malaria. Also what a pirate gets if he eats a particularly strong pickled onion.

WALK THE PLANK ~
Real pirates didn't really do this, they made it up for films and books. Real pirates like stabbin' and garottin'.

WEEVILS ~
These crunchy beetles would be found upon biting into the biscuits and bread on board.
You would be assured of weevil free hardtack if the biscuit was covered in large white maggots called 'bargemen'. They could be easily brushed off the top for a quick munching.
Pretty disgusting, but the lesser of two weevils!

WENCH ~
Women (of all kinds)

YELLOW JACK ~
Flag raised to warn others of disease on
board. Also used as a cheeky way of
keeping enemies away.

YO - HO - HO ~
Robert Louis Stephenson wrote this first
in Treasure Island and I don't think
pirates would ever say this, Santa maybe,
but not pirates. ARRRRR!

ZEE ~
A French man might say, "Oh no, zee
pirates are coming!"

☠

All of the following everyday phrases
originated from sea faring terms.

At a loose end
rigging becoming untied.

Shut your gob / gobbie
A gob line is used to pull in the towrope
and would take a lot of concentration
to get this right.

Chock-a-block
Pulley blocks are tackle used for
hauling cargo on board ship. They are
also used during bad weather to hold
down the items on deck normally stored
in wooden crates or 'chocks'.
If there was a large amount of cargo
being stored on deck it would be
'chock-a-block'.

How are you bearing up?
Bear= sail with the wind.

Dingbat
Badly made mop or 'swab'.

Dogsbody
The hardest and virtually inedible
hardtack would be passed down to the
lowest ranked member of the crew.
They would pulp this down with water
to create a nearly edible dish called
'dogsbody'.

Fall foul of
To crash your ship.

Flogging a dead horse
'Dead horse time' is the period after
being paid in advance for a month.
As the crew would normally spend their
pay quickly on extra rum and weapons
they felt working during this time was
like flogging a dead horse.

Give a dog a bad name
When piracy was rife, you could claim
any old sea-dog you had fallen out with
was a pirate. The government would
execute anyone looking sea-doggish
without much evidence.
So it was an easy way of removing your
enemies by giving them a bad name.

Keep mum
Pirates took the dice game 'mumchance' very seriously and kept silent or 'mum' during the game.
'Keep stumm' came from when they were playing really drunk and slurring.

Lifeline
If you happen to go overboard for any reason to 'grab a lifeline' would be to hoist yourself back on board with one of the ropes trailing into the sea.

Pipe down
If there was any noise or chatter below decks after boatswain's pipe had been blown you would be told to 'pipe down', if you didn't do this you might get keelhauled.

Rub salt into the wound
For an extra punishment salt would be rubbed into your gashes after a fierce flogging.

Sling your hook
Hammocks would have to be rolled tightly so they could be neatly stowed into a hooked loop on the wall during battle. If a rubbish pirate couldn't get his to fit he would be told to put it elsewhere or 'sling your hook'.

'Sling your daniel' was also an expression used for a sailor that hadn't packed his bag up tightly enough. He would normally end up stashing his pack or 'daniel' in a bilge ridden area.

Snot
Very high winds were known as 'snotters'
and the rather unhealthy young boys on
board would annoy the captains by wiping
their noses on their sleeves during
this bad weather.

This was solved by sewing three sharp
buttons on the sleeves so that the
'snotty little oinks' would be slightly
less dirty.

Take it easy ~
To haul in the sails slowly and carefully.

Drift ~
The direction of a ship going by wind or
tide.
'Do you get my drift?'

☠

ON BEING MORE PIRATE-LIKE

Now you can walk the walk, but can you
talk the talk?
Add what you have learned from
the dictionary to these tips and
ye'll be talkin' pirate in nay time.

Try and say AARRRR or YAARG before
anything you say.

I be = I am

Ye' be= you are

Ne'er say any V's

Or any G's

Pirates never say thank you,
the politer pirate may softly say
'yaaarrrr' with a slight nod of the head.

☠

Refer to people older than you or in positions of power as laddie or lassie.

Try throwing some insults in at the end.

Say bastard <u>A LOT</u>

Some examples:

"Watch out there's a car coming."
=
"Car Ahoy ye' blind bilge-bag."

"Yes thanks mum, I'd love a cup of tea."
=
" I be wantin' rum or nowt' ye' hairy faced bastard!"

"Hi there, how are you?"
=
"AARRR" (answer to the question is normally AARRR).

"I am going to Spain on my holidays."
=
"Yarr I be sailin' off to Spainardland to get meself a wench."

"Do you fancy coming to the pub tonight?"
=
"Get yer' parrot lovin' scurvy bones out of the hammock, we be splicing the main brace tonight!"

"Could you please tell me where the nearest toilets are?"
=
"Steer me smartly toward th' shitter 'fore I loose me cargo!"

"Excuse me waiter can we have our bill please?"
=
"Gimme more rum or ye'll be eating yer' own lips!"

Now you can talk the talk, but how do you introduce yourself at a dinner party?

It's time to FIND OUT YOUR PIRATE NAME, follow the steps and find your true pirate alias.

TAKE THE FIRST LETTER OF YOUR FIRST NAME.

A = IRON

B = LONG

C = LAZY

D = MAD

E = SIR

F = SEAMAN

G = BOOZY

H = SKIPPER

I = DIRTY

J = CAPTAIN

K = CORSAIR

L = HAIRY

For example, if your first name is Jimmy your new first pirate name is Captain.

M = OLD

N = FANCY

O = FIRSTMATE

P = SWABBIE

Q = BIG

R = ANGRY

S = BLOODY

T = DREADFUL

U = SOGGY

V = PRIVATEER

W = BRAVE

XYZ = GROWLIN'

☠

NOW CHANGE THE FIRST LETTER
OF YOUR SURNAME

A = DAVEY   G = JIM

B = JEFF   H = GEORGE

C = WILDMAN   I = GREG

D = ROGER   J = BART

E = BILLY   K = EDRIG

F = RED   L = JACK

For example, if your surname is Williams the next part of your new pirate name is Thomas.

M = JOHN	**S = REX**
N = BRODERICK	**T = JOHN-PAUL**
O = WEEVIL	**U = BRIAN**
P = CRAZY-EYE	**V = SILAS**
Q = DON	**W = THOMAS**
R = JAKE	**XYZ = SHIRLEY**

NOW CHANGE THE LAST LETTER
OF YOUR SURNAME

A = DIRTY-SAILS   G = SCURVY-FACE

B = RUSTY-BLADE   H = DEAD-PARROT

C =BARNACLE-TOE   I = BRAVE-FACE

D =BLACKBEARD   J = HOOK-HAND

E = BRIGHT-BLADE   K= CRUSTY-PLANK

F =COLD-HEART   L = RATFACE

So Jimmy Williams is now called CAPTAIN THOMAS BIG-SWAGGER.

M = PEG-LEG

N = DARKMANE

O =BISCUIT

P=GINGERBEARD

Q = MORGAN

R =WILDBLOOD

S = BIG-SWAGGER

T= SHARP-SWORD

U= PUGWASH

V = RACKHAM

W= BLUEBEARD

XYZ =SMYTHE

NOW THAT YOU HAVE A FITTING NAME, WHY NOT CHANGE YOUR CAR / BIKE / SKATEBOARD / TRUCK'S NAME TO ONE OF THESE TO ADD TO THE EFFECT?

BACHELOR'S DELIGHT
BLACK JOKE
CHARMING MARY
PRIVATEER'S DESIRE
DARK REVENGER
DOLPHIN'S DESIRE
FLYING DRAGON
GOOD FORTUNE
HAPPY DELIVERY
MAYFLOWER
MOST HOLY TRINITY

☠

NIGHT RAMBLER
REVENGE
RISING SUN
ROYAL FORTUNE
SEA KING
SNAP DRAGON
SPEEDY RETURN
SUDDEN DEATH
VICTORY O' THE SEAS

ALWAYS refer to your vehicle as 'her',
'she', 'my beauty' or 'me beast o' the seas.'

Before you know it people will be saying
"Wow! Here comes Boozy Jake Morgan
sailin' in on the Flying Dragon."

☠

"Get the grog ready, we be splicing the mainbrace tonight"

Pirate Jokes

(Traditionally unfunny)

Pirate one:
"AARR, why has ye' got the ships wheel down the front of yer' trousers?"
Pirate two:
"I don't know but it's drivin' me nuts!"

What do you call 1000 pirates in a room?
- Avast conspiracy!

How many pirates does it take to change a light bulb?
- None, they like it in the daaarrk.

Pirate one:
"That be a fine looking hook and peg leg ye' got for yerself."
Pirate two:
" I should think so, they cost me an arm and a leg!"

How do pirates navigate their ships?
- With the staaarrs!

What do you call an angry man with a hook and a parrot?
- An irate pirate.

What do sea monsters eat?
- Fish and ships!

Pirate one:
"So how did you lose yer' eye then matey?"
Pirate two:
"A bastard seagull did a dirty big shit in it."
Pirate one :
"'tis the strangest thing I ever heard, a man blinded with seagull shit!"
Pirate two:
" Not really, 'twas me first day with me new hook!"

Why did the pirate become a boxer?
Because he had a good right hook.

Why do pirates hate circles?
- 'Cos they be scurvy!

Why did the seagull blush?
- Because the seaweed.

Pirate one:
"That be a fine new ship yer' got yerself,
be it economic?
Pirate two:
"YAARR, it does 100 miles to
the galleon."

To make your own pirate jokes simply use any word with the letters AR in it, and work from there, some examples:

Where does a pirate do his shopping?
- AAAARRRgos.

What is a pirate's favourite designer label?
- AAAARRRmarni.

What is a pirate's favourite style of the late 19th century?
- AAAARRRt nouveau.

Where do pirate penguins live?
- In the AAAARRRctic.

Where does a pirate process his photographs?
- In a dAAAARRRk room.

What is a pirate's favourite 80's band?
- AARRR~HARRRR!

The possibilities are endless......

☠

82

Pirate Recipes

(Not for fussy eaters)

Mainly living on a diet of rum, fish
and biscuits,
the ship's cook would knock up these
treats when they had nicked enough
ingredients from sailors and islanders.

SALAMUNGI
Pirate salad
2 oz pickled beef
1 fresh rat or sea bird
Handful of anchovies
2 Eggs (cackle farts)
Roughly chop ingredients with an axe.
Place in mixing bowl and drizzle with oil
and vinegar.
Serve with rum.

HARD TACK
Ship's biscuits
2 tankards flour
1 tankard water
Check flour for weevil larvae.
Mix water and flour to make dough.
Pinch of salt to taste.
Cook at 250 degrees for 7 hours until
rock hard and inedible.
(Will keep for 3~4 months)
Serve with rum.

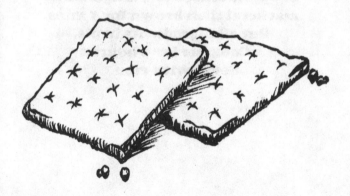

☠

SEAGULL PIE
<u>Filling, yet disgusting</u>
3 large onions
4 seagulls (dead)
Mackerel
2 tankards flour
Water
**Make a pie base with the flour
and water and bake.
Chop the onions and seagulls and
mackerel then brown for 5 mins.
Put all ingredients in pie.
Cook pie for 2 hours.
Serve with rum.**

LOBSCOUSE
Traditional stew
2 onions
1 goat
Pickled vegetables
Sauté the onion and goat.
Add water, salt and other ingredients.
Bring to the boil then simmer for 9/10
hours until meat is tender.
Serve with rum.

SCOTTISH DUFF
Pirate pudding
10 oz beef suet
2 cups flour
Sugar, cinnamon and spices to taste
Molasses
Syrup
1 egg
Biscuit crumbs.
4 bananas
Mix up ingredients and place on canvas,
tie up tightly and boil for 3 hours.
Serve with rum.

Top Ten Secret Celebrity Pirates

1 / BRIAN BLESSED
He might know but he's not letting on.

2/ LAURENCE LLEWELYN~BOWEN
Bi~pirate~curious.

3/ BRIAN MAY
Stick an eye patch on him and he's done.

4/ MICHAEL BOLTON
How can we be lovers if we can't be pirates?

5/ JEREMY PAXMAN
Keeps his parrot under the Newsnight desk.

6/ CHUCK NORRIS
Not many pirates have hairy ginger backs, but this one does!

7/ CHARLOTTE CHURCH
Voice of an angel, Heart of a pirate.

8/ HUGH FEARNLEY~WHITTINGSTALL
Only a man with a pirate's soul could eat his own pets.

9/ JOHN PRESCOTT
Looks like a pirate, fights like a pirate.

10/ GABRIELLE

TOP TEN PIRATE POP ACTS

1
AAARRR KELLY

2
DR HOOK

3
PILLAGE PEOPLE

4
RUM DMC

5
PLANK SINATRA

6
DEXY'S MIDNIGHT RUDDERS

7
BUOY ZONE

8
STONE TEMPLE PIRATES

9
AARRCTIC MONKEYS

10
FALL OUT BUOY

Pirate
Chat up
Lines

YE' CAN WALK ME PLANK ANYTIME

Your cabin or mine?

I be sure ye' 'ave some real treasure in that thar' chest.

☠

Be that a hornpipe in ye' pocket or is ye' pleased to see me

Gaze deeply into my one eye and you'll see me love be as deep as the ocean

YE' BE THE PRETTIEST BARNACLE-FREE BEAUTY OF ALL THE ISLANDS.

Ye' be lookin' as swell as the ocean!

ARRRR me name's Roger, wanna make me jolly?

IF YE' BE A LUCKY LASS YE' CAN POLISH ME CUTLASS.

Well shiver me timber and blow me down!

Do ye' mind if the parrot watches...?

Pirate
Insults

Ye' lily~Livered land lubber!

SUCK ON A LEMON YE' SCURVY DOG.

Ye' son of a biscuit eater!

Yer' vessel be as barnacle ridden as Ye' mother!

I BEEN LOOKIN' FOR A SUNKEN
CHEST AND ALL ME FOUND
WAS YER' WIFE!

**ARRR me hearty, I
be smellin' ye' mouldy
hull from 'ere.**

*Ne'er before did I see
such a lice-infested
bilge rat!*

I'll foul on ye' gibbet, ye' yellow~bellied swine.

Gangway ye' pox~faced blowfish, yer' parrot looks as green as ye'!

☠

Ye' be smellin' worse than a poop deck on a hot sailin' day!

☠

Personality Test

(See if you've got a bit of pirate in you)

**Answer the following questions
as honestly as you can to see
if you have got what it takes to
start a life of piracy.**

**What is the first thing you do when you
wake up in the morning?**

a- Rub your eyes and yawn
b- Scratch your bum and fart
c- Check your biscuits for weevils

How would you describe your ideal day?

a- A picnic in the park followed by
   some kitten stroking
b- A bottle of cider in the park
   followed by a game of knock down
   ginger
c- A bottle of rum on the poop deck
   followed by some swashbuckling

Describe yourself in three words

    a- **Cheerful, bright and fun**
    b- **Cool, funny and adventurous**
    c- **Gruff, hard~drinking and immoral**

What is your favourite colour?

    a- **Pink**
    b- **Black**
    c- **Blood**

Can you pat your head and rub your tummy at the same time?

    a~ **yes**
    b~ **no**
    c~ **I've got a hook for a hand and I'm holding my cutlass in the other one, do you think I'm stupid, YAAAARRRRR!**

Describe your favourite meal.

- a- Smoked salmon salad and a guava smoothie
- b- Pot noodle and a can of lager
- c- Pickled rats and a bottle of rum

Where do you see yourself in 25 years time?

- a- Settled down in a country cottage with horses and children
- b- Still surfing the internet for obscure porn
- c- Roaming the seas as a pirate ghost AAARRG!

☠

If you answered MOSTLY A's

~ Nice try but not the makings of a
pirate. You seem far too lovely for
cold~blooded murder, robbery and
hard~drinking. Try growling at random
strangers in the supermarket and only
consuming mackerel and rum for a week.
You might then be on the right road to
Pirateville.

If you answered MOSTLY B's
~ You are currently an urban pirate but
have the makings of a true swashbuckler.
However, a life of piracy is not a decision
to be taken lightly. Why not try getting a
job on a cruise ship and see how you feel?

☠

If you answered MOSTLY C's

~ **You are a dirty, dirty pirate. Well done.**

Thanks for reading ye' bastards!

Special thanks to the following shipmates.

Neil Williams for his amazing skull and cutlass design.

Rob and Lou, who know the difference between Old English and old English!

Paul Whiteside, who can draw a barnacle like no man on earth.

☠